The New Mediterranean Diet Cookbook 2021

Everything You Need To Know About The Mediterranean Diet With Easy, Quick And Affordable Recipes To Help You Reset Your Metabolism And Change Your Eating Habits

Mediterranean Recipes America

© Copyright 2021 - All rights reserved.

Table of contents

Introduction

About the Mediterranean Diet

Transitioning into the Mediterranean diet is mainly about bracing yourself for a new way of eating, adapting your attitude toward food into one of joyful expectation and appreciation of good meals and good company. It's like a mindset as anything else, so you'll want to make your environment unite so you can quickly adapt to the lifestyle in the Mediterranean way.

Benefits of the Mediterranean Diet

Boosts Your Brain Health: Preserve memory and prevent cognitive decline by following the Mediterranean diet that will limit processed foods, refined bread, and red meats. Have a glass of wine versus hard liquor.

Improves Poor Eyesight: Older individuals suffer from poor eyesight, but in many cases, the Mediterranean diet has provided notable improvement. An Australian Center for Eye Research discovered that the individuals who consumed a minimum of 100 ml (0.42 cup) of olive oil weekly were almost 50% less likely to develop macular degeneration versus those who ate less than one ml each week.

Helps to Reduce the Risk of Heart Disease: The New England Journal of Medicine provided evidence in 2013 from a randomized clinical trial. The trial was implemented in Spain, whereas individuals did not have cardiovascular disease at enrollment but were in the 'high risk' category. The incidence of major cardiovascular events was reduced by the Mediterranean diet that was supplemented with extra-virgin olive oil or nuts. In one study, men who consumed fish in this manner reduced the risk by 23% of death from heart disease.

The Risk of Alzheimer's disease is reduced: In 2018, the journal Neurology studied 70 brain scans of individuals who had no signs of dementia at the onset. They followed the eating patterns in a two-year study resulting in individuals who were on the Med diet had a lesser increase of the depots and reduced energy use - potentially signaling risk for Alzheimer's.

Helps Lessen the Risk of Some Types of Cancer: According to the results of a group study, the diet is associated with a lessened risk of stomach cancer (gastric adenocarcinoma).

Decreases Risks for Type 2 Diabetes: It can help stabilize blood sugar while protecting against type 2 diabetes with its low-carb elements. The Med diet maintains a richness in fiber, which will digest slowly while preventing variances in your blood sugar. It also can help you maintain a healthier weight, which is another trigger for diabetes.

Suggests Improvement for Those with Parkinson's disease: By consuming foods on the Mediterranean diet, you add high levels of antioxidants that can prevent your body from undergoing oxidative stress, which is a damaging process that will attack your cells. The menu plan can reduce your risk factors in half.

Mediterranean Diet Pyramid

The Mediterranean Diet Pyramid is a nutritional guide developed by the World Health Organization, Harvard School of Public Health, and Oldways Preservation Trust in 1993. It is a visual tool that summarizes the Mediterranean diet, suggested eating patterns, and guides how frequently specific mechanisms should be eaten. It allows you to break healthy eating habits and not overfill yourself with too many calories.

Olive oil, fruits, vegetables, whole grains, legumes, beans, nuts & seeds, spices & herbs: These foods form the Mediterranean pyramid base. If you did observe, you would notice that these are mostly from plant sources. You should try and include a few variations of these items into each meal you eat. Olive oil should be the primary fat in cooking your dishes and endeavor to replace any other butter or cooking oil you may have been using to cook.

Fish & seafood: These are essential staples of the Mediterranean diet that should be consumed often as a protein source. You would want to include these in your diet at least two times a week. Try new varieties of fish, either frozen or fresh. Also, incorporate seafood like mussels, crab, and shrimp into your diet. Canned tuna is also great to include on sandwiches or toss in a salad with fresh vegetables.

Cheese, yogurt, eggs & poultry: These ingredients should be consumed in more moderate amounts. Depending on the food, they should be used sparingly throughout the week. Keep in mind that if you are using eggs in baking or cooking, they will also be counted in your weekly limit. You would want to stick to more healthy cheese like Parmesan, ricotta, or feta that you can add a topping or garnish on your dishes.

Red meat & sweets: These items are going to be consumed less frequently. If you are going to eat them, you need to consume only small quantities, most preferably lean meat versions with less fat when possible. Most studies recommend a maximum of 12 to 16 ounces per month. To add more variety to your diet, you can still have red meat occasionally, but you would want to reduce how often you have it. It is essential to limit its intake because of all the health concerns of sugar and red meat. The Mediterranean diet improves cardiovascular health and reduces blood pressure, while red meat tends to be dangerous to your cardiovascular system. The Greece population ate very little red meat and instead had fish or seafood as their main protein source.

Water: The Mediterranean diet encourages you to stay hydrated.

Wine: Moderate consumption of wine with meals is encouraged on the Mediterranean diet. Studies shown that moderate consumption of alcohol can reduce the risk of heart disease. That can mean about 1 glass per day for women. Men tend to have higher body mass so that they can consume 1 to 2 drinks. Please keep in mind what your doctor would recommend regarding wine consumption based on your health and family history.

10 Tips for Success

The healthy Mediterranean way of life is about eating balanced foods rich in vitamins, minerals, antioxidants, and healthy fatty acids. However, the Mediterranean diet is just one aspect of it. The Mediterranean way of life calls for regular physical exercise, plenty of rest, healthy social interaction, and fun. Balancing all these aspects was the secret of the excellent health of the Mediterranean folk back in the day. However, only the Mediterranean diet is the primary focus of this book, and we will spend most of our time talking about just that.

1. Eat Healthy Fats

The Mediterranean diet is not low-fat diet at all, but the fat included in this diet is considered healthy for the body, and the heart in particular. Remember: not all fats are created equal. Certain kinds of fats are beneficial, while others do more harm than good. Monosaturated fats and polyunsaturated omega-3 fatty acids, for example, are considered healthy. Omega-6 polyunsaturated fatty acids and saturated fats are unhealthy, and these harmful fats are primarily present in most of the typical food worldwide. The United States, for example, absolutely loves saturated fats. According to a survey, saturated fats constitute 11% of an average American's total calories, which is a very high number compared to an average Mediterranean resident, who consumes less than 8% of his/her calories through saturated fat. If you wish to switch to the healthy Mediterranean way of life, the first thing to do is change the oils you consume. Eliminating fats like butter and lard in favor of more nourishing oils like olive oil would be the place to start.

2. Consume Dairy in Moderation

We all love cheese. Dairy products are delicious, nutritious, and excellent sources of calcium and should be consumed in moderation if you're following the Mediterranean diet. It is usually a good idea to drink two to three servings of full-fat dairy products in a single day, where one serving can mean an 8-ounce glass of milk, or an ounce of cheese or 8 ounces of yogurt.

3. Consume Tons of Plant-Based Foods

As we saw in the pyramid, fruits, vegetables, legumes, and whole grains form the basis of the Mediterranean diet. So, it is a good idea to eat five to ten servings of these in a single day, depending on your appetite. Eat as many as you want, but don't overeat. Plant-based foods are naturally low in calories and high in fiber and nutrients. Fresh, unprocessed plants are best, so always be on the lookout for the best sources of these around you!

4. Spice Things Up with Fresh Spices and Herbs

Fresh herbs and spices make most of the recipes insanely delicious while also providing health benefits. If you already use these in your daily cooking, more power to you! If not, we got you covered!

5. Consume Seafood Weekly and Meat Monthly

As we've talked about before, one benefit of living close to the sea is easy access to seafood. However, seafood holds a lower priority than plant-based foods in the Mediterranean diet and should be consumed in moderation. If you're a vegetarian, consider taking fish oil supplements to get those omega-3 fatty acids into your system.

Consume Meat Monthly: Red meat used to be a luxury for the Mediterranean people back in the day. Although not completely off-limits, you should try and reduce your red-meat intake as much as possible. If you love red meat, consider consuming it no more than two times per month. And even when you eat it, make sure the serving size of the meat in the dish is small (two to three-ounce serving). The main reason to limit meat intake is to limit the number of unhealthy fats going into your system. As we talked before, saturated fats and omega-6 fatty acids are not suitable for health, but unfortunately, red meat contains significant quantities. As a beef lover myself, I eat a two-ounce serving of it per month, and when I do eat it, I make sure there are lots of vegetables on the side to satiate my hunger.

6. Work Your Body

Now you don't have to hit the gym like a maniac to work your body. Walking to your destination instead of driving, taking the stairs instead of the lift, or kneading your dough can all get the job done. So, be creative and work your body when you can. Better yet, play a sport or just hit the gym like a maniac. You don't have to, as I said at the start, but it will help… a lot.

7. Enjoy a Big Lunch

Lunch was usually the meal of the day when the Mediterranean residents sat with their families and took their time enjoying a big meal. This strengthens social bonds and relaxes the mind during the most stressful time of the day, when you're just halfway done with your work, probably.

8. Have Fun with Friends and Family

Just by spending time and doing something fun with your loved ones is great for de-stressing. Today, we don't understand the importance of this, and people feel lonely, and in some cases, even depressed. Just doing this one thing has the power to solve a huge chunk of the problems our modern society faces.

9. Be Passionate

The Mediterranean people are passionate folk. Living on or close to sun-kissed coasts, their passion for life is naturally high. Being passionate about something in life can take you a long way towards health and wellness.

10. Planning Your Meals

If you're a beginner and have not yet made the switch to the Mediterranean diet, you will need to identify what changes you need to make to your current diet to make it match closely with the Mediterranean diet. In time, the Mediterranean diet will come to you naturally, but to start, you will need to plan. You will need to plan your portion sizes, and how often you eat certain foods. The changes are small but will benefit you in the long run.

Appetizer and Snack Recipes

1. Grilled Spiced Turkey Burger

Preparation Time: 15 minutes - Cooking Time: 20 minutes

Serving: 3

Size/ Portion: 1 burger

Ingredients:

- Onion (1.8 oz, chopped fine)

- Extra Virgin Olive Oil (1/3 tbsp)

- Turkey (14.4 oz, ground)

- Salt (1/3 tbsp)

- Curry powder (1/3 tbsp)

- Lemon zest (2/5 tsp, grated)

- Pepper (1/8 tsp)

- Cinnamon (1/8 tsp)

- Coriander (1/4 tsp, ground)

- Cumin (1/8 tsp, ground)

- Cardamom (1/8 tsp, ground)

- Water (1.2 Fl oz)

- Tomato Raisin Chutney (as desired)

- Cilantro leaves (as desired)

Directions:

1. Cook the onions in the oil. Cool completely.

2. Combine the turkey, onions, spices, water, and salt in a bowl. Toss.

3. Divide the mixture into 5 oz portions (or as desired). Form each portion into a thick patty.

4. Broil but do not overcook it.

5. Plate the burgers. Put spoonful of chutney on top of each.

Nutrition:

250 Calories

14g Fat 27g Protein

2. Tomato Tea Party Sandwiches

Preparation Time: 15 minutes

Cooking Time: 0 minute

Serving: 4

Size/ Portion: 1 sandwich

Ingredients:

- Whole wheat bread (4 slices)

- Extra virgin olive oil (4 1/3 tbsp)

- Basil (2 1/8 tbsp., minced)

- Tomato slices (4 thick)

- Ricotta cheese (4 oz)

- Dash of pepper

Directions:

1. Toast bread to your preference.

2. Spread 2 tsp. olive oil on each slice of bread. Add the cheese.

3. Top with tomato, then sprinkle with basil and pepper.

4. Serve with lemon water and enjoy it!

Nutrition:

239 Calories

16.4g Fat

6g Protein

3. Veggie Shish Kebabs

Preparation Time: 10 minutes

Cooking Time: 0 minute

Serving: 3

Size/ Portion: 3 pieces

Ingredients:

- Cherry tomatoes (9) Mozzarella balls (9 low-fat)

- Basil leaves (9) Olive oil (1 tsp.)

- Zucchini (3, sliced)

- Dash of pepper

For Serving:

- Whole Wheat Bread (6 slices)

Directions:

1. Stab 1 cherry tomato, low-fat mozzarella ball, zucchini, and basil leaf onto each skewer.

2. Situate skewers on a plate and drizzle with olive oil. Finish with a sprinkle of pepper.

3. Set your bread to toast. Serve 2 bread slices with 3 kebobs.

Nutrition:

349 Calories

5.7g Fat

15g Protein

4. Lemon Fat Bombs

Preparation Time: 10 minutes - Cooking Time: 0 minutes

Servings: 3

Ingredients:

- 1 whole lemon 4 ounces cream cheese

- 2 ounces butter   2 teaspoons natural sweetener

Directions:

1. Take a fine grater and zest your lemon. Squeeze lemon juice into a bowl alongside the zest. Add butter, cream cheese to a bowl, and add zest, salt, sweetener, and juice.

2. Stir well using a hand mixer until smooth. Spoon mix into molds and freeze for 2 hours. Serve and enjoy!

Nutrition:

Calories: 404 Carbs: 4g Fiber: 1g Protein: 4g

Fat: 43g Sodium: 19 mg

Breakfast Recipes

5. Menemen

Preparation Time: 6 minutes

Cooking Time: 15 minutes

Servings: 4

Size/ Portion: 1 cup

Ingredients

- 2 tomatoes, chopped

- 2 eggs, beaten

- 1 bell pepper, chopped

- 1 teaspoon tomato paste

- ¼ cup of water

- 1 teaspoon butter

- ½ white onion, diced

- ½ teaspoon chili flakes

- 1/3 teaspoon sea salt

Directions

1. Melt butter in the pan.

2. Add bell pepper and cook it for 3 minutes over the medium heat. Stir it from time to time.

3. After this, add diced onion and cook it for 2 minutes more.

4. Stir the vegetables and add tomatoes.

5. Cook them for 5 minutes over the medium-low heat.

6. Then add water and tomato paste. Stir well.

7. Add beaten eggs, chili flakes, and sea salt.

8. Stir well and cook Menemen for 4 minutes over the medium-low heat.

9. The cooked meal should be half runny.

Nutrition:

67 Calories

3.4g fat 3.8g protein

6. Watermelon Pizza

Preparation Time: 10 minutes

Cooking Time: 0 minute

Servings: 3

Size/ Portion: 3 wedges

Ingredients

- 9 oz watermelon slice

- 1 tablespoon Pomegranate sauce

- 2 oz Feta cheese, crumbled

- 1 tablespoon fresh cilantro, chopped

Directions

1. Place the watermelon slice in the plate and sprinkle with crumbled Feta cheese.

2. Add fresh cilantro.

3. After this, sprinkle the pizza with Pomegranate juice generously.

4.   Cut the pizza into the servings.

Nutrition:

143 Calories

6.2g fat

5.1g protein

7. Ham Muffins

Preparation Time: 10 Minutes

Cooking Time: 15 minutes

Servings: 4

Size/ Portion: 1

Ingredients

- 3 oz ham, chopped

- 4 eggs, beaten

- 2 tablespoons coconut flour

- ½ teaspoon dried oregano

- ¼ teaspoon dried cilantro

Directions

1.   Spray the muffin's molds with cooking spray from inside.

2.   In the bowl mix up together beaten eggs, coconut flour, dried oregano, cilantro, and ham.

3.   When the liquid is homogenous, pour it in the prepared muffin molds.

4.   Bake the muffins for 15 minutes at 360 °F.

5.   Chill the cooked meal well and only after this remove from the molds.

Nutrition:

128 Calories

7.2g fat

10g protein

8. Savory Yogurt Bowls

Preparation time: 15 minutes Cooking time: 0 minutes

Servings:4

Ingredients:

- 1 medium cucumber, diced ½ cup pitted Kalamata olives, halved 2 tablespoons fresh lemon juice

- 1 tablespoon extra-virgin olive oil

- 1 teaspoon dried oregano ¼ teaspoon freshly ground black pepper 2 cups nonfat plain Greek yogurt ½ cup slivered almonds

Directions:

1. In a small bowl, mix the cucumber, olives, lemon juice, oil, oregano, and pepper. Divide the yogurt evenly among 4 storage containers. Top with the cucumber-olive mix and almonds.

Nutrition: Calories: 240 Fat: 16g Carbohydrates: 10g Protein: 16g Potassium: 353mg Sodium: 350mg

9. Energy Sunrise Muffins

Preparation time: 15 minutes

Cooking time: 25 minutes

Servings: 16

Ingredients:

- Nonstick cooking spray

- 2 cups whole wheat flour

- 2 teaspoons baking soda

- 2 teaspoons ground cinnamon

- 1 teaspoon ground ginger

- ¼ teaspoon salt

- 3 large eggs

- ½ cup packed brown sugar

- 1/3 cup unsweetened applesauce

- ¼ cup honey

- ¼ cup vegetable or canola oil

- 1 teaspoon grated orange zest

- Juice of 1 medium orange

- 2 teaspoons vanilla extract

- 2 cups shredded carrots

- 1 large apple, peeled and grated

- ½ cup golden raisins

- ½ cup chopped pecans

- ½ cup unsweetened coconut flakes

Directions:

1. If you can fit two 12-cup muffin tins side by side in your oven, then leave a rack in the middle, then preheat the oven to 350°F.

2. Coat 16 cups of the muffin tins with cooking spray or line with paper liners. Mix the flour, baking soda, cinnamon, ginger, and salt in a large bowl. Set aside.

3. Mix the eggs, brown sugar, applesauce, honey, oil, orange zest, orange juice, and vanilla until combined in a medium bowl. Add the carrots and apple and whisk again.

4. Mix the dry and wet ingredients with a spatula. Fold in the raisins, pecans, and coconut. Mix everything once again, just until well combined. Put the batter into the prepared muffin cups, filling them to the top.

5. Bake within 20 to 25 minutes, or until a wooden toothpick inserted into the middle of the center muffin comes out clean (switching racks halfway through if baking on 2 racks). Cool for 5 minutes in the tins, then transfers to a wire rack to cool for an additional 5 minutes. Cool completely before storing in containers.

Nutrition:

Calories: 292 Fat: 14g

Carbohydrates: 42g

Protein: 5g

Sodium: 84mg

10. Spinach, Egg, And Cheese Breakfast Quesadillas

Preparation time: 15 minutes

Cooking time: 15 minutes

Servings: 4

Ingredients:

- 1½ tablespoons extra-virgin olive oil

- ½ medium onion, diced

- 1 medium red bell pepper, diced

- 4 large eggs

- 1/8 teaspoon salt

- 1/8 teaspoon freshly ground black pepper

- 4 cups baby spinach

- ½ cup crumbled feta cheese

- Nonstick cooking spray

- 4 (6-inch) whole-wheat tortillas, divided

- 1 cup shredded part-skim low-moisture mozzarella cheese, divided

Directions:

Warm-up oil over medium heat in a large skillet. Add the onion and bell pepper and sauté for about 5 minutes, or until soft.

1. Mix the eggs, salt, and black pepper in a medium bowl. Stir in the spinach and feta cheese. Put the egg batter in the skillet and scramble for about 2 minutes, or until the eggs are cooked. Remove from the heat.

2. Coat a clean skillet with cooking spray and add 2 tortillas. Place one-quarter of the spinach-egg mixture on one side of each tortilla. Sprinkle each with ¼ cup of mozzarella cheese. Fold the other halves of the tortillas down to close the quesadillas and brown for about 1 minute.

3. Turnover and cook again in a minute on the other side. Repeat with the remaining 2 tortillas and ½ cup of mozzarella cheese. Cut each quesadilla in half or wedges. Divide among 4 storage containers or reusable bags.

Nutrition:

Calories: 453

Fat: 28g

Carbohydrates: 28g

Fiber: 4.5g

Protein: 23g

Potassium: 205mg

Sodium: 837mg

Main Dish Recipes

11. High-Quality Belizean Chicken Stew

Preparation Time: 7 minutes

Cooking Time: 23 minutes

Servings: 4

Size/ Portion: 2 cups

Ingredients

- 4 whole chicken

- 1 tablespoon coconut oil

- 2 tablespoons achiote seasoning

- 2 tablespoons white vinegar

- 3 tablespoons Worcestershire sauce

- 1 cup yellow onion, sliced

- 3 garlic cloves, sliced

- 1 teaspoon ground cumin

- 1 teaspoon dried oregano

- ½ teaspoon black pepper

- 2 cups chicken stock

Directions

1. Take a large sized bowl and add achiote paste, vinegar, Worcestershire sauce, oregano, cumin and pepper. Mix well and add chicken pieces and rub the marinade all over them

2. Allow the chicken to sit overnight. Set your skillet to Sauté mode and add coconut oil

3. Once hot, cook chicken pieces to the skillet in batches. Remove the seared chicken and transfer them to a plate

4. Add onions, garlic to the skillet and Sauté for 2-3 minutes. Add chicken pieces back to the skillet

5. Pour chicken broth to the bowl with marinade and stir well. Add the mixture to the skillet

6. Seal up the lid and cook for about 20 minutes at high pressure

7. Once done, release the pressure naturally. Season with a bit of salt and serve!

Nutrition:

517 calories

21g fats

9g protein

12. Crispy Mediterranean Chicken Thighs

Preparation Time: 9 minutes

Cooking Time: 35 minutes

Servings: 6

Size/ Portion: ½ lbs.

Ingredients:

- 2 tablespoons extra-virgin olive oil

- 2 teaspoons dried rosemary

- 1½ teaspoons ground cumin

- 1½ teaspoons ground coriander

- ¾ teaspoon dried oregano

- 1/8 teaspoon salt 6 chicken thighs (about 3 pounds)

Directions

1. Preheat the oven to 450 °F. Line a baking sheet with parchment paper.

2. Place the olive oil and spices into a large bowl and mix together, making a paste. Add the chicken and mix together until evenly coated. Place on the prepared baking sheet.

3. Bake for 30 to 35 minutes.

Nutrition:

491 calories

22g fats

10g protein

13. Greek Penne and Chicken

Preparation Time: 11 minutes

Cooking Time: 9 minutes

Servings: 4

Size/ portion: 4 ounces

Ingredients

- 16-ounce package of Penne Pasta

- 1-pound Chicken Breast Halves

- 1/2 cup of Chopped Red Onion

- 1 1/2 tablespoons of Butter

- 2 cloves of Minced Garlic

- 14-ounce can of Artichoke Hearts

- 1 Chopped Tomato

- 3 tablespoons of Chopped Fresh Parsley

- 1/2 cup of Crumbled Feta Cheese

- 2 tablespoons of Lemon Juice

- 1 teaspoon of Dried Oregano

- Ground Black Pepper

- Salt

Directions:

1. In a large sized skillet over a medium-high heat, melt your butter. Add your garlic and onion. Cook approximately 2 minutes. Add your chopped chicken and continue to cook until golden brown. Should take approximately 5 to 6 minutes. Stir occasionally.

2. Reduce your heat to a medium-low. Drain and chop your artichoke hearts. Add them to your skillet along with your chopped tomato, fresh parsley, feta cheese, dried oregano, lemon juice, and drained pasta. Cook for 2 to 3.

3. Season. Serve!

Nutrition: 411 calories 20g fats 8g protein

Side Recipes

14. Springtime Quinoa Salad

Preparation Time: 10 minutes

Cooking Time: 25 minutes

Serving: 4

Size/ portion: 2 cups

Ingredients

for vinaigrette:

- 1 pinch of salt

- 1 pinch of black pepper

- ½ teaspoon of dried thyme

- ½ teaspoon of dried oregano

- ¼ cup of extra-virgin olive oil

- 1 tablespoon of honey

- juice of 1 lemon

- 1 clove of garlic, minced

- 2 tablespoons of fresh basil, diced

for salad:

- 1 ½ cups of cooked quinoa

- 4 cups of mixed leafy greens

- ½ cup of kalamata olives, halved and pitted

- ¼ cup of sun-dried tomatoes, diced

- ½ cup of almonds, raw, unsalted and diced

Directions:

1.   Combine all the vinaigrette ingredients together, either by hand or using a blender or food processor. Set the vinaigrette aside in the refrigerator.

2.   In a large salad bowl, combine the salad ingredients.

3.   Drizzle the vinaigrette over the salad, then serve.

Nutrition:

201 calories 13g fat 4g protein

15. Seafood Souvlaki Bowl

Preparation Time: 20 minutes

Cooking Time: 20 minutes

Serving: 4

Size/ Portion: 2 cups

Ingredients

for salmon

- 1 pinch of salt

- 1 pinch of black pepper

- 1 tablespoon of fresh oregano

- 1 tablespoon of paprika

- 1 tablespoon of fresh dill

- 3 tablespoons of extra-virgin olive oil

- 2 tablespoons of balsamic vinegar

- 6 tablespoons of freshly squeezed lemon juice

- 2 cloves of garlic, minced

- 1 lb. of fresh salmon, cut into 4 fillets

Ingredients:

- 1 pinch of salt

- 1 pinch of black pepper

- 2 tablespoons of extra-virgin olive oil

- Juice of 1 lemon

- 2 red bell peppers, diced

- 1 large cucumber, diced 1 zucchini, sliced

- 1 cup of cherry tomatoes, halved

- ½ cup of kalamata olives, pitted and halved

- 1 cup of dry pearled couscous8 oz. of feta, cubed

Directions:

1. Cook the couscous following the package instructions and set aside.

2. In a medium mixing bowl, add all the souvlaki ingredients apart from the fish. Combine well, then coat each fish fillet. Allow the fillets to rest in the bowl for 15 minutes.

3. In a separate mixing bowl, combine the sliced bell peppers and zucchini. Add two tablespoons of olive oil, salt, and pepper. Combine and set aside.

4. In a medium skillet over medium heat, cook the salmon until tender, then remove from the heat.

5. Add the sliced peppers and zucchini to the skillet and cook for three minutes until you see charring, then remove from the heat.

6. To serve, dish the couscous up into four serving bowls and top with the lemon juice. Add the cooked salmon, charred vegetables, cucumber, tomatoes, olives, and feta.

Nutrition:

159 calories 11g fat 2g protein

16. Lime Carrots

Preparation time: 10 minutes Cooking time: 30 minutes

Servings: 4

Ingredients:

- 1-pound baby carrots, trimmed 1 tablespoon sweet paprika

- 1 teaspoon lime juice   3 tablespoons olive oil

- A pinch of black pepper 1 teaspoon sesame seeds

Directions:

1. Arrange the carrots on a lined baking sheet, add the paprika and the other ingredients except for the sesame seeds, toss, bake at 400 °F within 30 minutes. Divide the carrots between plates, sprinkle sesame seeds on top and serve as a side dish.

Nutrition:

Calories 139 Protein 1.1g Carbohydrates 10.5g Fat 11.2g

4g fiber Sodium 89mg Potassium 313mg

17. Garlic Potato Pan

Preparation time: 10 minutes

Cooking time: 1 hour

Servings: 8

Ingredients:

- 1-pound gold potatoes, peeled and cut into wedges

- 2 tablespoons olive oil 1 red onion, chopped

- 2 garlic cloves, minced

- 2 cups coconut cream

- 1 tablespoon thyme, chopped

- ¼ teaspoon nutmeg, ground

- ½ cup low-fat parmesan, grated

Directions:

1. Warm-up a pan with the oil over medium heat, put the onion plus the garlic, and sauté for 5 minutes. Add the potatoes and brown them for 5 minutes more.

2. Add the cream and the rest of the ingredients, toss gently, bring to a simmer and cook over medium heat within 40 minutes more. Divide the mix between plates and serve as a side dish.

Nutrition:

Calories 230

Protein 3.6g

Carbohydrates 14.3g

Fat 19.1g

Fiber 3.3g

Cholesterol 6mg

Sodium 105mg

Potassium 426mg

18. Balsamic Cabbage

Preparation time: 10 minutes

Cooking time: 20 minutes

Servings: 4

Ingredients:

- 1-pound green cabbage, roughly shredded

- 2 tablespoons olive oil

- A pinch of black pepper

- 1 shallot, chopped

- 2 garlic cloves, minced

- 2 tablespoons balsamic vinegar

- 2 teaspoons hot paprika 1 teaspoon sesame seeds

Directions:

1. Heat-up a pan with the oil over medium heat, add the shallot and the garlic, and sauté for 5 minutes. Add the cabbage and the

other ingredients, toss, cook over medium heat for 15 minutes, divide between plates and serve.

Nutrition:

Calories 100

Protein 1.8g

Carbohydrates 8.2g

Fat 7.5g

Fiber 3g

Sodium 22mg

Potassium 225mg

Seafood Recipes

19. Spiced Swordfish

Preparation Time: 10 minutes

Cooking Time: 15 minutes

Servings: 4

Size/ Portion: 7 ounces

Ingredients:

- 4 (7 ounces each) swordfish steaks

- 1/2 teaspoon ground black pepper

- 12 cloves of garlic, peeled

- 3/4 teaspoon salt

- 1 1/2 teaspoon ground cumin

- 1 teaspoon paprika

- 1 teaspoon coriander

- 3 tablespoons lemon juice

- 1/3 cup olive oil

Directions:

1. Take a blender or food processor, open the lid and add all the ingredients except for swordfish. Close the lid and blend to make a smooth mixture. Pat dry fish steaks; coat evenly with the prepared spice mixture.

2. Add them over an aluminum foil, cover and refrigerator for 1 hour. Preheat a griddle pan over high heat, pour oil and heat it. Add fish steaks; stir-cook for 5-6 minutes per side until cooked through and evenly browned. Serve warm.

Nutrition

255 Calories

12g Fat

0.5g Protein

20. Anchovy Pasta Mania

Preparation Time: 10 minutes

Cooking Time: 20 minutes

Servings: 4

Size/ Portion: 1 fillet

Ingredients:

- 4 anchovy fillets, packed in olive oil

- ½ pound broccoli, cut into 1-inch florets

- 2 cloves garlic, sliced   1-pound whole-wheat penne

- 2 tablespoons olive oil   ¼ cup Parmesan cheese, grated

- Salt and black pepper, to taste

- Red pepper flakes, to taste

Directions:

1. Cook pasta as directed over pack; drain and set aside. Take a medium saucepan or skillet, add oil. Heat over medium heat.

2. Add anchovies, broccoli, and garlic, and stir-cook until veggies turn tender for 4-5 minutes. Take off heat; mix in the pasta. Serve warm with Parmesan cheese, red pepper flakes, salt, and black pepper sprinkled on top.

Nutrition

328 Calories

8g Fat

7g Protein

Vegetable Recipes

21. Cauliflower Steaks with Eggplant Relish

Preparation Time: 5 minutes

Cooking Time: 25 minutes

Serving: 4

Size/ Portion: ½ lb.

- 2 small heads cauliflower ¼ teaspoon kosher or sea salt

- ¼ teaspoon smoked paprika extra-virgin olive oil, divided

- 1 recipe Eggplant Relish Spread

Direction:

1. Situate large, rimmed baking sheet in the oven. Set oven to 400 °F with the pan inside.

2. Stand one head of cauliflower on a cutting board, stem-end down. With a long chef's knife, slice down through the very center of the head, including the stem. Starting at the cut edge, measure about 1 inch and cut one thick slice from each cauliflower half, including as much of the stem as possible, to

make two cauliflower "steaks." Reserve the remaining cauliflower for another use. Repeat with the second cauliflower head.

3. Dry each steak well with a clean towel. Sprinkle the salt and smoked paprika evenly over both sides of each cauliflower steak.

4. Put skillet over medium-high heat, cook 2 tablespoons of oil. When the oil is very hot, add two cauliflower steaks to the pan and cook for about 3 minutes. Flip and cook for 2 more minutes. Transfer the steaks to a plate. Wipe out the pan to remove most of the hot oil. Repeat the cooking process with the remaining 2 tablespoons of oil and the remaining two steaks.

5. Using oven mitts, carefully remove the baking sheet from the oven and place the cauliflower on the baking sheet. Roast in the oven for 13 minutes. Serve with the Eggplant Relish Spread.

Nutrition:

282 calories 22g Fat 8g Protein

22. Mediterranean Lentil Sloppy Joes

Preparation Time: 5 minutes

Cooking Time: 15 minutes

Serving: 4

Size/ Portion: 2 cups

Ingredients:

- 1 tablespoon extra-virgin olive oil

- 1 cup chopped onion

- 1 cup chopped bell pepper

- 2 garlic cloves

- 1 (15-ounce) can lentils, drained and rinsed

- 1 (14.5-ounce) can low-sodium tomatoes

- 1 teaspoon ground cumin

- 1 teaspoon dried thyme

- ¼ teaspoon kosher or sea salt

- 4 whole-wheat pita breads, split open

- 1½ cups chopped seedless cucumber

- 1 cup chopped romaine lettuce

Direction

1. In a saucepan at medium-high heat, sauté onion and bell pepper for 4 minutes. Cook garlic and stir in lentils, tomatoes (with their liquid), cumin, thyme, and salt.

2. Turn the heat to medium and cook, stirring occasionally, for 10 minutes.

3. Stuff the lentil mixture inside each pita. Lay the cucumbers and lettuce on top of mixture and serve.

Nutrition:

334 Calories

5g Fat

16g Protein

23. Stuffed Tex-Mex Baked Potatoes

Preparation time: 15 minutes

Cooking time: 45 minutes

Servings: 2

Ingredients:

- 2 large Idaho potatoes

- ½ cup black beans, rinsed and drained

- ¼ cup store-bought salsa 1 avocado, diced

- 1 teaspoon freshly squeezed lime juice

- ½ cup nonfat plain Greek yogurt

- ¼ teaspoon reduced-sodium taco seasoning

- ¼ cup shredded sharp cheddar cheese

Directions:

1. Preheat the oven to 400 °F. Scrub the potatoes, then slice an "X" into the top of each using a paring knife. Put the potatoes on the oven rack, then bake for 45 minutes until they are tender.

2. In a small bowl, stir the beans and salsa and set aside. In another small bowl, mix the avocado and lime juice and set aside. In a third small bowl, stir the yogurt and the taco seasoning until well blended.

3. When the potatoes are baked, carefully open them up. Top each potato with the bean and salsa mixture, avocado, seasoned yogurt, and cheddar cheese, evenly dividing each component, and serve.

Nutrition:

Calories: 624

Fat: 21g

Carbohydrates: 91g

Fiber: 21g

Protein: 24g

Sodium: 366mg

Potassium: 2134mg

24. Lentil-Stuffed Zucchini Boats

Preparation time: 15 minutes Cooking time: 45 minutes

Servings: 2

Ingredients:

- 2 medium zucchinis, halved lengthwise and seeded

- 2¼ cups water, divided

- 1 cup green or red lentils, dried & rinsed

- 2 teaspoons olive oil

- 1/3 cup diced onion 2 tablespoons tomato paste

- ½ teaspoon oregano ¼ teaspoon garlic powder

- Pinch salt ¼ cup grated part-skim mozzarella cheese

Directions:

1. Preheat the oven to 375 °F. Line a baking sheet with parchment paper. Place the zucchini, hollow sides up, on the baking sheet, and set aside.

2. Boil 2 cups of water to a boil over high heat in a medium saucepan and add the lentils. Lower the heat, then simmer within 20 to 25 minutes. Drain and set aside.

3. Heat-up the olive oil in a medium skillet over medium-low heat. Sauté the onions until they are translucent, about 4 minutes. Lower the heat and add the cooked lentils, tomato paste, oregano, garlic powder, and salt.

4. Add the last quarter cup of water and simmer for 3 minutes, until the liquid reduces and forms a sauce. Remove from heat.

5. Stuff each zucchini half with the lentil mixture, dividing it evenly, top with cheese, bake for 25 minutes and serve. The zucchini should be fork-tender, and the cheese should be melted.

Nutrition:

Calories: 479 Fat: 9g Carbohydrates: 74g

Fiber: 14g Protein: 31g

Sodium: 206mg Potassium: 1389mg

Soup and Stew Recipes

25. Classic Chicken Soup

Preparation Time: 10 minutes

Cooking Time: 25 minutes

Servings: 2

Size/ Portion: 1 cup

Ingredients:

- 1 1/2 cups low-sodium vegetable broth

- 1 cup of water

- 1/4 teaspoon poultry seasoning

- 1/4 teaspoon black pepper 1 cup chicken strips

- 1/4 cup carrot   2-ounces egg noodles, uncooked

Directions:

1. Gather all the ingredients into a slow cooker and toss it Cook soup on high heat for 25 minutes.

2. Serve warm.

Nutrition:

103 calories

8g protein

11g fat

26. Cucumber Soup

Preparation Time: 10 minutes

Cooking Time: 0 minute

Servings: 4

Size/ Portion: 1 cup

Ingredients:

- 2 medium cucumbers

- 1/3 cup sweet white onion

- 1 green onion

- 1/4 cup fresh mint

- 2 tablespoons fresh dill

- 2 tablespoons lemon juice

- 2/3 cup water

- 1/2 cup half and half cream

- 1/3 cup sour cream

- 1/2 teaspoon pepper

- Fresh dill sprigs for garnish

Directions:

1. Situate all of the ingredients into a food processor and toss. Puree the mixture and refrigerate for 2 hours. Garnish with dill sprigs. Enjoy fresh.

Nutrition:

77 calories

2g protein

6g fats

27. Ham and Pea Soup

Preparation time: 15 minutes Cooking time: 8 hours

Servings: 8

Ingredients:

- 1 lb. Split Peas (dried) 1 cup sliced Celery

- 1 cup sliced Carrots 1 cup sliced Onion

- 2 cups chopped ham (cooked) 8 cups of water

Directions:

1. Place all the listed fixing in the slow cooker. Cook on "high" within 4 hrs. Serve hot.

Nutrition:

- Calories 118.6 Fat 1.9 g

- Cholesterol 15.9 mg Sodium 828.2 mg

- Carbohydrates 14.5 mg Fiber 5.1 g

- Protein 11.1 g

28. Pea Soup

Preparation time: 15 minutes Cooking time: 8 hours

Servings: 8

Ingredients:

- 16 oz. Split Peas (dried) 1 cup chopped Baby Carrots

- 1chopped onion (white) 3 Bay Leaves

- 10 oz. cubed Turkey Ham 4 cubes Chicken Bouillon

- 7 cups of water

Directions:

1. Rinse and drain peas. Place all the fixing in the slow cooker. Cook on "low" for 8 hrs. Serve hot.

Nutrition:

Calories 122.7 Fat 2 g Cholesterol 24 mg

Sodium 780.6 mg Carbohydrates 15 mg

Fiber 5.2 g Protein 11.8 g

Vegetarian Recipes

29. Buttered Fava Beans

Preparation Time: 30 minutes

Cooking Time: 15 minutes

Serving: 4

Size/ Portion: ½ cup

Ingredients

- ½ cup vegetable broth

- 4 pounds fava beans

- ¼ cup fresh tarragon

- 1 teaspoon chopped fresh thyme

- ¼ teaspoon black pepper

- 1/8 teaspoon salt

- 2 tablespoons butter

- 1 garlic clove, minced

- 2 tablespoons chopped fresh parsley

Direction:

1. In a shallow pan over medium heat, bring the vegetable broth to a boil.

2. Add the fava beans, 2 tablespoons of tarragon, the thyme, pepper, and salt. Cook for 10 minutes.

3. Stir in the butter, garlic, and remaining 2 tablespoons of tarragon. Cook for 2 to 3 minutes.

4. Sprinkle with the parsley.

Nutrition:

458 calories

9g fat

37g protein

30. Freekeh

Preparation Time: 10 minutes

Cooking Time: 40 minutes

Serving: 4

Size/ portion: ½ cup

Ingredients:

- 4 tablespoons Ghee

- 1 onion, chopped

- 3½ cups vegetable broth

- 1 teaspoon ground allspice

- 2 cups freekeh

- 2 tablespoons pine nuts

Direction

1. In a heavy-bottomed saucepan over medium heat, melt the ghee.

2. Stir in the onion and cook for about 5 minutes, stirring constantly, until the onion is golden.

3. Pour in the vegetable broth, add the allspice, and bring to a boil.

4. Stir in the freekeh and return the mixture to a boil. Reduce the heat to low, cover the pan, and simmer for 30 minutes, stirring occasionally.

5. Spoon the freekeh into a serving dish and top with the toasted pine nuts.

Nutrition:

459 calories

18g fat

19g protein

Salad Recipes

31. Apples and Pomegranate Salad

Preparation Time: 10 minutes Cooking Time: 0 minutes

Servings: 4 Size/ Portion: 2 cups

Ingredients:

- 3 big apples, cored and cubed

- 1 cup pomegranate seeds

- 3 cups baby arugula 1 cup walnuts, chopped

- 1 tablespoon olive oil 1 teaspoon white sesame seeds

- 2 tablespoons apple cider vinegar

Directions:

1. Mix the apples with the arugula and the rest of the ingredients in a bowl, toss and serve cold.

Nutrition: 160 Calories 4.3g Fat 10g Protein

Dessert Recipes

32. Strawberries Coconut Cake

Preparation Time: 10 minutes

Cooking Time: 25 minutes

Servings: 6

Size/ portion: 1 slice

Ingredients:

- 2 cups almond flour

- 1 cup strawberries, chopped

- ½ teaspoon baking soda

- ½ cup coconut sugar

- ¾ cup coconut milk

- ¼ cup avocado oil

- 2 eggs, whisked

- 1 teaspoon vanilla extract

- Cooking spray

Directions:

1. In a bowl, combine the flour with the strawberries and the other ingredients except the cooking spray and whisk well.

2. Grease a cake pan with cooking spray, pour the cake mix, spread, bake in the oven at 350 °F for 25 minutes, cool down, slice and serve.

Nutrition:

465 calories

22g fat

13.4g protein

Lunch

33. Creamy Chicken Breast

Preparation time: 10 minutes

Cooking time: 20 minutes

Servings: 4

Ingredients:

- 1 tablespoon olive oil A pinch of black pepper

- 2 pounds chicken breasts, skinless, boneless, and cubed

- 4 garlic cloves, minced

- 2 and ½ cups low-sodium chicken stock

- 2 cups coconut cream ½ cup low-fat parmesan, grated

- 1 tablespoon basil, chopped

Directions:

1. Heat-up a pan with the oil over medium-high heat, add chicken cubes, and brown them for 3 minutes on each side. Add garlic, black pepper, stock, and cream, toss, cover the pan and cook

everything for 10 minutes more. Add cheese and basil, toss, divide between plates and serve for lunch. Enjoy!

Nutrition:

Calories 221

Fat 6g

Fiber 9g

Carbs 14g

Protein 7g

Sodium 197 mg

Dinner

34. Shrimp Cocktail

Preparation time: 10 minutes

Cooking time: 5 minutes

Servings: 8

Ingredients:

- 2 pounds big shrimp, deveined

- 4 cups of water

- 2 bay leaves

- 1 small lemon, halved

- Ice for cooling the shrimp

- Ice for serving

- 1 medium lemon sliced for serving

- ¾ cup tomato passata

- 2 and ½ tablespoons horseradish, prepared

- ¼ teaspoon chili powder

- 2 tablespoons lemon juice

Directions:

1. Pour the 4 cups water into a large pot, add lemon and bay leaves. Boil over medium-high heat, reduce temperature, and boil for 10 minutes. Put shrimp, stir and cook within 2 minutes. Move the shrimp to a bowl filled with ice and leave aside for 5 minutes.

2. In a bowl, mix tomato passata with horseradish, chili powder, and lemon juice and stir well. Place shrimp in a serving bowl filled with ice, with lemon slices, and serve with the cocktail sauce you've prepared.

Nutrition:

Calories: 276

Carbs: 0g

Fat: 8g

Protein: 25g

Sodium: 182 mg

Mains

35. Spicy Tofu Burrito Bowls with Cilantro Avocado Sauce

Preparation time: 15 minutes

Cooking time: 15 minutes

Servings: 4

Ingredients:

For the sauce:

- ¼ cup plain nonfat Greek yogurt

- ½ cup fresh cilantro leaves

- ½ ripe avocado, peeled

- Zest and juice of 1 lime

- 2 garlic cloves, peeled

- ¼ teaspoon kosher or sea salt

- 2 tablespoons water

For the burrito bowls:

- 1 (14-ounce) package extra-firm tofu

- 1 tablespoon canola oil

- 1 yellow or orange bell pepper, diced

- 2 tablespoons Taco Seasoning

- ¼ teaspoon kosher or sea salt

- 2 cups Fluffy Brown Rice

- 1 (15-ounce) can black beans, drained

Directions:

1. Place all the sauce ingredients in the bowl of a food processor or blender and purée until smooth. Taste and adjust the seasoning, if necessary. Refrigerate until ready for use.

2. Put the tofu on your plate lined with a kitchen towel. Put another kitchen towel over the tofu and place a heavy pot on top, changing towels if they become soaked. Let it stand within

15 minutes to remove the moisture. Cut the tofu into 1-inch cubes.

3. Warm-up canola oil in a large skillet over medium heat. Add the tofu and bell pepper and sauté, breaking up the tofu into smaller pieces for 4 to 5 minutes. Stir in the taco seasoning, salt, and ¼ cup of water. Evenly divide the rice and black beans among 4 bowls. Top with the tofu/bell pepper mixture and top with the cilantro avocado sauce.

Nutrition:

Calories: 383

Fat: 13g

Sodium: 438mg

Carbohydrate: 48g

Protein: 21g

36. Sweet Potato Cakes with Classic Guacamole

Preparation time: 15 minutes

Cooking time: 20 minutes

Servings: 4

Ingredients:

For the guacamole:

- 2 ripe avocados, peeled and pitted

- ½ jalapeño, seeded and finely minced

- ¼ red onion, peeled and finely diced

- ¼ cup fresh cilantro leaves, chopped

- Zest and juice of 1 lime

- ¼ teaspoon kosher or sea salt

For the cakes:

- 3 sweet potatoes, cooked and peeled

- ½ cup cooked black beans

- 1 large egg

- ½ cup panko bread crumbs

- 1 teaspoon ground cumin

- 1 teaspoon chili powder

- ½ teaspoon kosher or sea salt

- ¼ teaspoon ground black pepper

- 2 tablespoons canola oil

Directions:

1. Mash the avocado, then stir in the jalapeño, red onion, cilantro, lime zest and juice, and salt in a bowl. Taste and adjust the seasoning, if necessary.

2. Put the cooked sweet potatoes plus black beans in a bowl and mash until a paste form. Stir in the egg, bread crumbs, cumin, chili powder, salt, and black pepper until combined.

3. Warm-up canola oil in a large skillet at medium heat. Form the sweet potato mixture into 4 patties, place them in the hot skillet,

and cook within 3 to 4 minutes per side, until browned and crispy. Serve the sweet potato cakes with guacamole on top.

Nutrition:

Calories: 369

Fat: 22g

Sodium: 521mg

Carbohydrate: 38g

Protein: 8g

Fish

37. Halibut in Parchment with Zucchini, Shallots, and Herbs

Preparation time: 15 minutes Cooking time: 15 minutes

Servings: 4

Ingredients:

- ½ cup zucchini, diced small 1 shallot, minced

- 4 (5-ounce) halibut fillets (about 1 inch thick)

- 4 teaspoons extra-virgin olive oil ¼ teaspoon kosher salt

- 1/8 teaspoon freshly ground black pepper

- 1 lemon, sliced into 1/8 -inch-thick rounds 8 sprigs of thyme

Directions:

1. Preheat the oven to 450°F. Combine the zucchini and shallots in a medium bowl. Cut 4 (15-by-24-inch) pieces of parchment paper. Fold each sheet in half horizontally.

2. Draw a large half heart on one side of each folded sheet, with the fold along the heart center. Cut out the heart, open the parchment, and lay it flat.

3. Place a fillet near the center of each parchment heart. Drizzle 1 teaspoon olive oil on each fillet. Sprinkle with salt and pepper. Top each fillet with lemon slices and 2 sprigs of thyme. Sprinkle each fillet with one-quarter of the zucchini and shallot mixture. Fold the parchment over.

4. Starting at the top, fold the parchment edges over, and continue all the way around to make a packet. Twist the end tightly to secure. Arrange the 4 packets on a baking sheet. Bake for about 15 minutes. Place on plates; cut open. Serve immediately.

Nutrition:

Calories: 190 Fat: 7g

Sodium: 170mg

Carbohydrates: 5g

Protein: 27g

38. Flounder with Tomatoes and Basil

Preparation time: 15 minutes

Cooking time: 20 minutes

Servings: 4

Ingredients:

- 1-pound cherry tomatoes

- 4 garlic cloves, sliced

- 2 tablespoons extra-virgin olive oil

- 2 tablespoons lemon juice

- 2 tablespoons basil, cut into ribbons

- ½ teaspoon kosher salt

- ¼ teaspoon freshly ground black pepper

- 4 (5- to 6-ounce) flounder fillets

Directions:

1. Preheat the oven to 425°F.

2. Mix the tomatoes, garlic, olive oil, lemon juice, basil, salt, and black pepper in a baking dish. Bake for 5 minutes.

3. Remove, then arrange the flounder on top of the tomato mixture. Bake until the fish is opaque and begins to flake, about 10 to 15 minutes, depending on thickness.

Nutrition:

Calories: 215

Fat: 9g

Sodium: 261mg

Carbohydrates: 6g

Protein: 28g

Poultry

39. Oven-Fried Chicken Breasts

Preparation time: 15 minutes Cooking time: 30 minutes

Servings: 8

Ingredients:

- ½ pack Ritz crackers 1 c. plain non-fat yogurt

- 8 boneless, skinless, and halved chicken breasts

Directions:

1. Preheat the oven to 350 °F. Rinse and pat dry the chicken breasts. Pour the yogurt into a shallow bowl. Dip the chicken pieces in the yogurt, then roll in the cracker crumbs. Place the chicken in a single layer in a baking dish. Bake within 15 minutes per side. Serve.

Nutrition:

Calories: 200 Fat:13 g Carbs:98 g Protein:19 g Sodium:217 mg

40. Rosemary Roasted Chicken

Preparation time: 15 minutes

Cooking time: 20 minutes

Servings: 8

Ingredients:

- 8 rosemary springs

- 1 minced garlic clove

- Black pepper

- 1 tbsp. chopped rosemary

- 1 chicken

- 1 tbsp. organic olive oil

Directions:

1. In a bowl, mix garlic with rosemary, rub the chicken with black pepper, the oil and rosemary mix, place it inside roasting pan, introduce inside the oven at 350 0F, and roast for sixty minutes

and 20 min. Carve chicken, divide between plates and serve using a side dish. Enjoy!

Nutrition:

Calories: 325

Fat:5 g

Carbs:15 g

Protein:14 g

Sodium: 950 mg

Conclusion

Congrats! Making this far on your MEDITERRANEAN-journey and embracing the MEDITERRANEAN diet as its best!

MEDITERRANEAN Diet has gained popularity in the past few years as it is beneficial in strengthening metabolism and controlling hypertension. Contrary to the popular belief that while following the MEDITERRANEAN diet, one gets to eat vegetarian foods while getting a balanced diet that includes fresh fruits, vegetables, nuts, low-fat dairy products, and whole grains. You do not have to cut down on meat; instead, you have to reduce sodium and fat content from your everyday diet.

The diet also has many health benefits as it helps reduce hypertension and obesity, lower osteoporosis, and prevent cancer. This well-balanced diet strengthens metabolism, which further helps in decomposing the fat deposits stored in the body. As a result, it improves and enhance the overall health of a person.

This cookbook has provided you different MEDITERRANEAN meals from breakfast, lunch, dinner, mains, side dishes, fish and seafood, poultry, vegetables, soups, salads, snacks, and desserts. However, you can consult experts if you suffer from current health conditions or follow certain exercise routines, as this will help you customize the diet as per your requirement.

This diet is easy to follow as you get to everything but in a healthier fashion and limited quantity. Talking about the MEDITERRANEAN diet outside the theory and more in practice reveals its efficiency as a diet. Besides excess research and experiments, the real reasons for people looking into this diet are its specific features. It gives the feeling of ease and convenience, making the users more comfortable with its rules and regulations.

Here are the following reasons why the MEDITERRANEAN Diet works amazingly:

Easy to Adopt: The broad range of options available under the MEDITERRANEAN diet label makes it more flexible for all. It is the reason that people find it easier to switch to and harness its real health benefits. It makes adaptability easier for its users.

Promotes Exercise: It is most effective than all the other factors because not only does it focus on the food and its intake, but it also duly stresses daily exercises and routine physical activities. It is the reason that it produces quick, visible results.

All-Inclusive: With a few limitations, this diet has taken every food item into its fold with certain modifications. It rightly guides about the Dos and Don'ts of all the ingredients and prevents us from consuming those harmful to the body and its health.

A Well-Balanced Approach: One of its most significant advantages is that it maintains balance in our diet, in our routine, our caloric intake, and our nutrition.